Have You Ever Wondered Who the One True God Really Is?

The one true God is a Spirit. He doesn't have a body like you and me. Even though you can't see God, He is everywhere. He sees and hears you. He knows what you are doing all the time.
God never had to learn; He knows everything. He knows more than the smartest man or woman.

God is the Creator. He made the world and everything in it—the mountains, the trees, the birds and animals. He made you and me too. We are His most special creation.

God could make all things because He is all powerful. He can do anything. Nothing is too hard for God.

God is holy. That means He is perfect—He never does anything that is not right and good.

God never changes—He will be the same forever and ever. God has prepared a perfect place called Heaven. It is a beautiful place where everything is good and right. God loves you and wants you to be with Him in Heaven too. His plan for you is found in His Word, the Bible.

" . . . I am God, and there is no other . . . there is none like me" (Isaiah 46:9).

Have You Ever Wondered What the Bible Is?

You may wonder who wrote the Bible, or if we can know that the Bible is really true. The Bible is a very special book from God. It is God's Word, and every word in the Bible is true. It is a most important book because it tells of God's plan for people. How do we know the Bible is God's book? God told 40 different men over a period of 1600 years to write down what He said to them. He guided the men in knowing what to say and how to say it. We don't know if God talked to them out loud or told them quietly in their thoughts.

God told the men to write down things that would happen in the future. Many of these things have already come true. All the rest of what the Bible says will come true as well.

There are 66 books in the Bible. They all agree and fit together perfectly. Only God could make a book like that! You and I can be sure that *all* of the Holy Bible is God's message to us—*every word!* Things around us don't last. But God's Word, the Bible, will last forever!

"All Scripture is God-breathed . . ." (2 Timothy 3:16).

Something to think about:

Who created the world and everything in it?

Connect the dots to see one way God speaks to us.

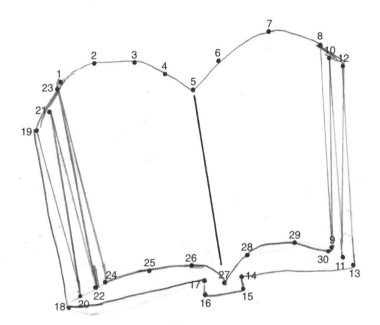

GOD'S BOOK

Prayer thought for the day:

God, help me as I learn more about Your book.

Have You Ever Wondered How the World Began?

Where did the world come from? Did it all happen by accident? Where did all of the people come from? The Bible tells us that God made all things. The Bible says, "In the beginning God created the heavens and the earth" (Genesis 1:1). God made the heavens—the sky, the stars and the sun. He also made the big round world we live in—the oceans, the mountains and the trees. Then God made animals. How powerful God is!

After God made the beautiful earth, He made one man. He made that man out of the dust of the earth and breathed life into him. God gave the man a soul that will live forever. He made man like Himself—although God is far greater. God called the man Adam. But Adam was alone. He needed someone who was made like him to be his friend and helper. God caused Adam to sleep and took a rib from his side. Out of Adam's rib God made the first woman. When Adam woke up, God gave him this woman to be his wife. Adam and Eve lived in a wonderful garden. Everything God made was very good. He is the great and wise Creator.

"You alone are the Lord. You made the heavens. . . . You give life to everything" (Nehemiah 9:6).

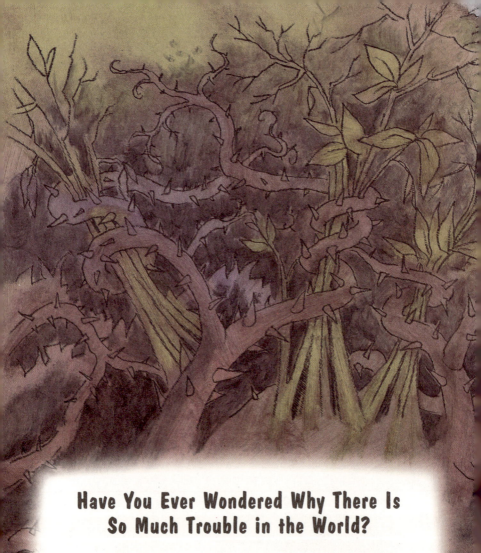

Have You Ever Wondered Why There Is So Much Trouble in the World?

Sometimes you may wonder why there is so much sadness in the world. Why do people get sick, and why do people hurt each other? When God made the world, He made everything beautiful and good. But many things in our world are not beautiful and good anymore. There is sickness and sadness, fighting and killing. Why did things go so wrong? It is because people did not obey God's laws. They sinned and spoiled God's perfect creation.

God had placed Adam and Eve in a beautiful garden and He told them they were not to eat the fruit from one certain tree or they would die. One day God's enemy Satan

tricked Eve into eating the fruit. Adam ate it too.
      In choosing to disobey God, both of them sinned. God told Adam and Eve that because they sinned they would have to leave the garden. The ground would grow weeds and thorns. They would have pain and sickness and their bodies would die. The worst thing about sin is that it separated Adam and Eve from God, who is holy and perfect. Everyone who would be born into the world after them would be born sinful and separated from God too. But God loved Adam and Eve. He promised them that one day a Savior would come to rescue the world from sin's punishment and bring us back to God.

> ". . . just as sin entered the world through one man, and death through sin, and in this way death came to all men, because all sinned" (Romans 5:12).

Something to think about:

God is so powerful. He alone created the world and everything in it.

Prayer thought for the day:

Thank Gód for His wonderful creation. Ask Him to help you understand who He is.

Have You Ever Wondered Why You Do Sinful Things?

Sometimes people wonder why they do wrong things when they know they should do what is right. What makes you and me want to sin? God has always had laws or rules for people to follow. But the very first people broke God's first rule. Ever since Adam and Eve chose to sin by disobeying God, each person has been born wanting to sin. Adam and Eve's children were born sinners, and you and I were also born wanting to sin.

What is sin? It is thinking, saying or doing things that break God's laws.

The Bible says, "For all have sinned and fall short of the glory of God" (Romans 3:23). No one is perfect like God. It is the sin in your heart that causes you to do bad things like lying, fighting or thinking mean things about someone else. There is no way for you to get rid of sin yourself. Only God can forgive your sin and take it away. It is important to let God forgive your sin because your sin keeps you away from Him. One day you will be separated forever from God in a terrible place of punishment unless your sin is forgiven.

". . . your iniquities [sins] have separated you from your God . . ." (Isaiah 59:2).

Have You Ever Wondered Why God Must Punish Sin?

  Do you know why sin is such a bad thing? God is holy. That means He is perfect and good. Because He is holy, He cannot let us do wrong without punishing us. If we sin against Him we deserve to be punished.
  Hundreds of years after Adam and Eve lived, there were many people on earth, and they were always doing sinful things. God was sad because of their sin and was sorry He had made them. They were making God's beautiful earth a terrible place.
  Then God said, "I will destroy man from the earth. I will put an end to their wickedness."

Only Noah and his family obeyed and pleased God. One day God told Noah that He was going to send a flood to cover the whole earth with water. The flood would be the punishment for the sinfulness of man.

God told Noah, "I want you to build an ark—a big boat. I will tell you exactly how large it should be and how to build it." Noah and his sons worked hard building the boat. They believed God. They told the people about the flood, but none of them believed Noah.

Finally, 120 years later, the ark was finished. Noah and his family went in with all the animals God wanted to save. God sent the flood and water covered the whole earth. All the wicked people were drowned. The holy God had punished them because of sin. Only those in the ark were saved.

God placed a rainbow in the sky to show that He would never again destroy the whole earth with a flood. Whenever you see a rainbow, you can remember two things: our holy God had to punish the wicked people for their sin and because Noah believed God, he and his family were saved from the flood. The promised Savior, or Messiah, would come through their family line.

". . .the wages of sin is death " (Romans 6:23).

Something to think about:

Road signs give us directions. If we miss a sign or don't pay attention, we can go the wrong way! The Bible tells us about people in the past, the present and the future to give us direction for our lives.

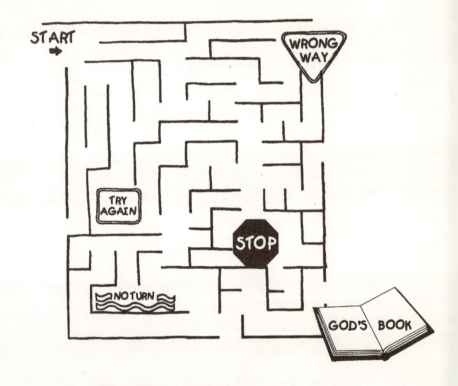

Prayer thought for the day:

Thank God for His promise to send a Savior to rescue the world from sin's punishment.

Have You Ever Wondered How God Kept His Promise to Send a Savior?

Even though God had to destroy the people in Noah's time because of sin, He provided the ark to save Noah's family. He also had a plan to save you and me, a plan to bring us back to Himself. Through Noah's family and those who were born after them, God planned to send the promised Savior. Finally, when the time was just right, God sent the Savior. That Savior was Jesus, God the Son.

Jesus came from Heaven to earth to be born as a tiny baby. God chose a young woman named Mary, who was a virgin, to give birth to His Son. Mary was an obedient young woman who found special favor in God's eyes. Without touching her in any physical way God placed the baby within her. It was a miracle! God gave Mary a husband named Joseph to help her take care of Jesus. As Jesus began to grow, He did things like you do. He went to school, He played with His friends, He helped His parents.

But there is one way in which Jesus was different from you and me. Jesus never sinned. Because He is the Son of God, He had no sin in His heart like we have when we are born. He never disobeyed His parents. He never disobeyed God, His Father, either. Jesus was perfect in every way.

"For the Son of Man [Jesus] came to seek and to save what was lost" (Luke 19:10).

Have You Ever Wondered How Jesus Showed That He Is God?

The miracle of Jesus' birth happened just as the prophets had said it would. Jesus is not like you and me, because He was born from the Spirit of God. There are other ways that Jesus is different also. Jesus is perfect. He never sinned in His words or His actions. He showed the people what God is like by doing miracles—healing people who were sick, helping blind people to see and crippled people to walk. He even brought some people who had died back to life again. Jesus fed over 5,000 people with a lunch a boy gave Him. Jesus spoke to a stormy sea and calmed the wind and waves.

Nothing was too hard for Him to do because Jesus is God. Jesus also showed people God's love.

He forgave people who were living sinful lives. He welcomed children into His arms to show that God loves children too.

Jesus taught how God wants people to think and behave. He said, "You must love the Lord your God with all your heart, all your soul and all your mind." And He said, "You must love your neighbor as yourself." Jesus also taught the people about God's plan for them to be saved from their sins by believing on Him as their Savior. Jesus obeyed God completely in everything He did and said. He was God the Son. But not everyone believed in Jesus. Some of the religious leaders became angry and jealous because the people loved and followed Jesus. So they made a plan to get rid of Him.

"For God so loved the world that he gave his one and only Son, that whoever believes in him shall not perish but have eternal life"
(John 3:16)

Something to think about:

Jesus was God's gift to the world to provide a way for anyone who believes in Him to be saved or forgiven of his sin.

Try to find your way through the maze to get to the gift in the middle.

Prayer thought for the day:

Thank God for sending this perfect gift to save the world from sin.

Have You Ever Wondered Why Jesus Is Called the Savior?

      Not just anyone could be our Savior. What did Jesus do to save you and me from our sin? One night, while Jesus was talking to His friends, the religious leaders sent a crowd with clubs and swords to arrest Him.
      "Lord, should we fight them?" His friends asked. "We have our swords!" And one of them cut off a servant's ear.
      But Jesus said, "Don't fight anymore." He touched the place where the man's ear had been and healed him.
      Quickly the guards grabbed Jesus and led Him to a ruler named Pilate. The religious leaders who hated Jesus put Him on trial and accused Him of things that weren't true. The soldiers hit Jesus, put a crown of thorns on His head and made fun of Him.

After Pilate questioned Jesus he said to the crowd, "This man is not guilty."

But the people yelled, "Away with Him! Crucify Him!" Then Pilate gave Jesus to them to be crucified—put to death on a cross.

Jesus hadn't done anything wrong. He was God the Son, the only perfect man without sin. But this was all part of God's plan. God was keeping His promise to provide a Savior.

". . .he humbled himself, and became obedient unto death. . ."
(Philippians 2:8).

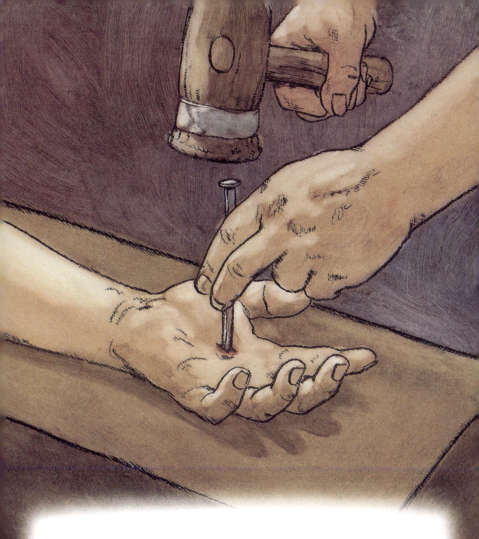

Have You Ever Wondered How Jesus Died?

You may not know how Jesus died, or even why a perfect man had to die at all. Jesus was taken to a place called Calvary to be crucified. Soldiers put nails through Jesus' hands and feet and hung Him on a cross. The people made fun of Him and said awful things. What pain and suffering! Blood came from His body.

As Jesus died on the cross that day, God placed upon Him the sin of the whole world. All the hatred, the lies, all the killing and wrong things ever done were put upon the Lord Jesus. He didn't deserve to die. He had no sin of His own, but He took your place on the cross.

The Bible says, "Without the shedding [giving] of blood there is no forgiveness" (Hebrews 9:22). If Jesus had not given His precious blood to take our punishment, we could never be forgiven of our sin.

At noontime as Jesus hung on the cross, darkness came over the whole countryside. Jesus cried out, "My God, My God, why have You forsaken Me?" The perfect, holy God could not look at His Son, who had taken upon Himself the sin of the world.

Later Jesus said, "Father, into Your hands I commit My spirit!" And Jesus died.

One of the soldiers who had seen all that had happened shouted, "Surely He is God's Son!"

When He took the punishment for sin on the cross, Jesus did all that was necessary to be called the Savior.

> "God made him [the Lord Jesus] who had no sin to be sin for us . . ." (2 Corinthians 5:21).

Something to think about:

Have you ever wanted to take the punishment for a friend because you loved him and didn't want to see him suffer? That's what Jesus did for you!

Color each space that has a dot in it.

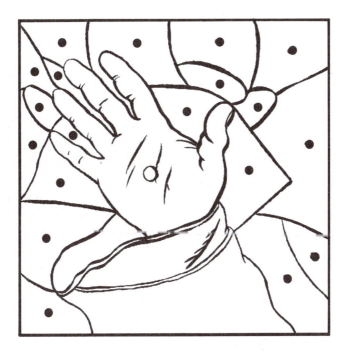

Prayer thought for the day:

Ask God to help you remember to talk to Him every day in prayer. He's always listening and He cares about you.

Have You Ever Wondered If Jesus Really Came Alive Again?

Jesus' followers buried His body in a tomb. Soldiers were ordered to guard it to make sure that no one would steal the body. Early on the first day of the week there was a great earthquake and an angel sent by God came and rolled back the stone from the door. The soldiers shook with fear and couldn't move or speak.

Some women who were friends of Jesus went to the tomb, bringing spices to put on Jesus' body. When they saw that the stone was rolled away, they hurried to look inside. And there they saw the angel.

The angel said, "Do not be afraid, for I know that you seek Jesus, who was crucified. He is not here; for He is risen as He said. Go quickly and tell His disciples that He is risen." The women ran to tell Jesus' friends, the disciples.

Later as the disciples were talking about it, Jesus Himself suddenly stood among them. He said, "Peace be with you." The disciples were afraid. But Jesus said, "Look at My hands. Look at

My feet. You can see that it is really Me. Touch Me so that you will know I am not a ghost."

Jesus was with His disciples for many weeks. More than 500 people saw Him and knew He had risen from the dead. Then one day when Jesus finished speaking with the disciples, they watched Him rise into the sky and disappear into a cloud. Jesus returned to Heaven where He is alive today.

By His great power God raised Jesus from the dead. He had kept His promise to pay for sin by sending His own beloved Son to be the Savior of the world.

". . . that Christ died for our sins according to the Scriptures [the Bible], that he was buried, that he was raised on the third day . . ."
(1 Corinthians 15:3-4).

Something to think about:

Why did Jesus have to die?

_____

_____

_____

_____

What happened after Jesus had been dead for three days?

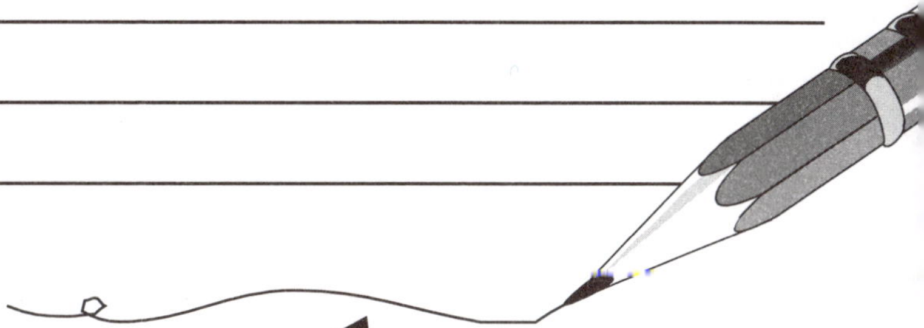

_____

_____

_____

_____

Prayer thought for the day:

Ask God to help you learn more about His wonderful gift.

Have You Ever Wondered How Jesus Can Become Your Personal Savior?

Now that you know that Jesus died for your sin, you may be wondering what you need to do to be forgiven. It is wonderful to know that Jesus died and came alive again for the sins of the whole world. But did you know that He died for *you*? Jesus wants to be your personal Savior. You can't save yourself from sin. You are not saved from sin's punishment by doing good things. You cannot be forgiven of your sins by saying prayers, giving money or trying to please God with your words or your actions. God says there is only one way, and that is through His Son, Jesus.

The Bible says, "Believe in the Lord Jesus, and you will be saved" (Acts 16:31). To believe means to trust completely in the Lord Jesus and become His follower. His death on the cross is the only payment for your sin that God will accept. When you choose to trust in the Lord Jesus as your personal Savior, God says you are saved. You are rescued from the punishment of your sin. You will not have to be separated from God in a place of punishment when you die. Instead you will be able to live with God forever in Heaven someday.

Would you like to believe on Jesus as your personal Savior and become His follower? You can tell God right now. You might pray something like this:

"Dear God, I know that I'm a sinner. I believe Your Son, Jesus, died to take the punishment for my sins. I believe You raised Him from the dead. I want the Lord Jesus to be my personal Savior and forgive my sins. Thank You for loving me and saving me from the punishment I deserve. In Jesus' name. Amen."

If you have truly put your trust in the Lord Jesus alone as your personal Savior, then God's promise to you is that you are saved. Your sins have been forgiven and Jesus has come to live in you by His Spirit.

"I [Jesus] am the way and the truth and the life. No one comes to the Father [God] except through me" (John 14:6).

Have You Followed God's Way to Be Forgiven?

Forgiven

3. Have you believed on the Lord Jesus as the only one who can forgive your sin?
yes____ no____

Color in the footprints showing each step you have taken to trust the Lord Jesus as your personal Savior.

START

1. Have you admitted that you are a sinner?
yes____ no____

SIN

You Can Know Jesus Has Saved You from Your Sin

Are you saved from the punishment of your sin? How do you know? We can read a verse in God's book, the Bible, that says, "Believe in the Lord Jesus, and you will be saved" (Acts 16:31). You can put your name in that verse: "If *(your name)* believes in the Lord Jesus, *(your name)* will be saved." If you truly believed (put your trust completely) in the Lord Jesus to forgive you, God has promised in the Bible that you have been saved from sin's punishment. God never lies—He never breaks His promises.

If you have put your trust in Jesus and become His follower, write the date in this space so you can always remember.

I trusted Jesus as my Savior_____.
(date)

Now that the Lord Jesus is your personal Savior, He has another promise for you. In the Bible God says, "I will never leave you" (Hebrews 13:5). You can put your name in place of "you." That means the Lord Jesus, who has come to live in you by His Spirit, will never go away from you. He will always be there to help you live for God and do what is right. In the very next verse God makes another promise to you: "The Lord is my helper" (Hebrews 13:6). What will God help you do? He will help you to obey Him and say no to God's enemy Satan. How wonderful to know for sure that Jesus has saved you from sin!

"I write these things to you who believe in the name of the Son of God so that you may know that you have eternal life . . ."
(1 John 5:13).

You Can Know You Have an Enemy

Satan is our greatest enemy. The Bible says that he was created by God as a beautiful angel. But he turned against God and wanted to destroy God's plan. He was the one who tricked Eve and brought sin into the world. Sin ruined God's beautiful creation.

Satan is also called the devil. From the beginning he wanted to stop God from keeping His promise to send a Savior to die for the sin of the whole world. But Satan failed. Jesus defeated Satan when He died on the cross and came alive from the dead.

Satan hates God and he hates those who have trusted the Lord Jesus as their own personal Savior.

Satan tries to make us do wrong things. He puts doubts and bad thoughts into our minds. He does not want us to love the Lord Jesus. If Jesus is your Savior, you do not have to be afraid of Satan. The Bible says, "The one [Holy Spirit] who is in you is greater than the one [Satan] who is in the world" (1 John 4:4). Jesus is God; He is greater and more powerful than Satan. Someday Satan and all those who follow him will be thrown into the lake of fire where they will be punished forever and ever. Since Jesus lives in you, you can learn how to win over your enemy Satan.

"Be self-controlled and alert. Your enemy the devil prowls around like a roaring lion looking for someone to devour." (1 Peter 5:8)

Something to think about:

How can you know your sin is forgiven?

When you do something wrong you should . . .

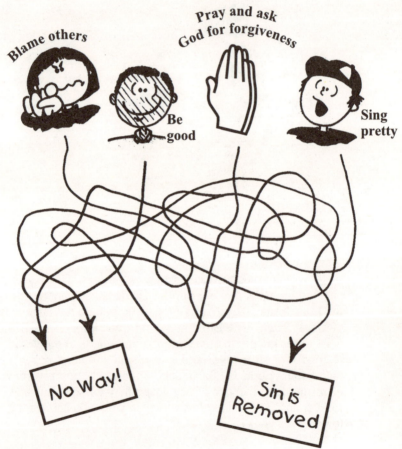

Prayer thought for the day:

Thank God that you are His child forever if you have asked Him to forgive you and save you. Your Heavenly Father loves you. Tell Him every time you do something wrong.

You Can Know How to Have Victory over Your Enemy

Can you really have victory over Satan every day? What happens if you fail? Satan wants you to sin so he can spoil your relationship with God. You need to remember four very important things that will help you have victory over Satan.

(1) You don't have to sin. Remember that the Lord Jesus already defeated Satan and sin when He died on the cross and rose again. The Bible says, "Resist [stand against] the devil, and he will flee [run] from you" (James 4:7). You can choose to say no to sin through the strength of the Lord Jesus, who lives in you.

(2) Remember that sin spoils your friendship with God. He will never leave you, but sin makes Him sad. Sin also blocks your prayers so that God will not answer.

(3) You can make things right by confessing your sin to God. The Bible says that if you agree with God about your sin, He is always fair and promises to forgive you. Then your friendship with God will be made right. Ask Him to help you not to sin that way again. You may also need to say "I'm sorry" to someone else who has been hurt by your sin.

(4) Thank God for victory over Satan. Remember that Jesus is the one who makes you a winner.

The Bible says, "Be strong in the Lord and in his mighty power" (Ephesians 6:10). How good it is to know deep inside that you can be a winner over Satan!

"But thanks be to God! He gives us the victory through our Lord Jesus Christ" (1 Corinthians 15:57).

You Can Know God Hears and Answers Prayer

What is prayer, and what can you pray about? Prayer is talking to God with your own thoughts or words, not just memorized phrases. He wants you to talk to Him each day. The Lord is never too busy to listen to your prayers.

You can talk to God anytime you want. The Bible says, "Pray continually" (1Thessalonians 5:17). You can pray when you're running and playing. Before you eat you can say, "Thank You, God, for this good food!" You can pray when someone is sick, "Dear God, please

help my friend get well." When you are afraid, ask God to take your fear away. You can also ask God help you learn more about Him.

God likes to hear about how you feel. Talk to Him when you are happy. Tell Him when you are sad. When you do wrong things, tell God you are sorry right away. He will always forgive you of your sin. Ask God to give you strength to do what is right.

God will *always* hear you when you pray. But He will not always give you what you ask for. Sometimes He says, "No, that is not good for you." Sometimes He says, "Yes." Sometimes He says, "Wait, not yet." But you can know one thing for sure, He will do what is best for you. Remember, God always hears and answers your prayers.

". . . in everything, by prayer and petition [asking], with thanksgiving, present your requests to God" (Philippians 4:6).

Something to think about:

You can have victory over sin. God promised us victory through our Lord Jesus Christ.

Prayer thought for the day:

Thank God for giving you His strength and power in the battle over sin.

You Can Get to Know God Better

Since you have believed on the Lord Jesus as your Savior, God wants you to get to know Him better. One way that you can do that is to spend some time each day reading the Bible and talking to Him in prayer. This is called your "quiet time."

You can decide on a certain time each day that will be your quiet time. Maybe it will be when you first wake up in the morning or just before bed at night. Think of a good place to have your quiet time—a place where others won't bother you.

Start your quiet time with a short prayer, asking God to help you understand and obey what He teaches you. Be sure that you have

also confessed your sin so that you are ready to learn and obey.

You may not have a Bible, but there are verses from the Bible in this book that you can read and memorize. Pick out a few verses and read them slowly and carefully. Some of the verses are promises for you to believe; some are commands for you to obey. Ask yourself what the words mean and how God wants you to obey. Spend a few minutes memorizing one verse each week so that you can say it without looking at it.

The last part of your quiet time is prayer. Talk to God about the verses you have just read. Ask Him to help you remember to obey His Word. Your prayer time can also include some of the other things you have already learned about prayer in this book. If you have a quiet time with God every day, you will get to know Him more and more. And the better you know God, the more like Him you will become.

"Evening, morning and noon I cry out . . . and he hears my voice" (Psalm 55:17).

You Can Know There Are Others Who Love Jesus Too

     Sometimes you may wonder if you are the only one who believes in Jesus. From the beginning of time there have always been people who have loved God and obeyed His Word. The moment you trusted the Lord Jesus as your Savior, you became part of God's family—a family of men and women and boys and girls who live all over the world. Those who belong to God should show love for each other.

     Usually members of God's family get together to have fellowship. They pray together and sing about God. They also study God's book, the Bible, to learn more about Him and how to help each other. Where do they get together? Believers sometimes meet in homes, outside or in buildings called churches.

     Remember, you are not the only one who has believed in Jesus as your Savior. There are probably some other people in your town or city who love Jesus too. You could ask God to lead you to another person who is a brother or sister in Christ.

"... As I have loved you, so you must love one another ..."
(John 13:34).

True or False?

1. A "quiet time" is reading a verse from the Bible and talking to God in prayer. _____
2. You can pray anywhere. _____
3. God can only hear you if you pray in the morning. _____
4. God always says yes to our prayers. _____
5. God cares about all of your problems. _____
6. You will get to know God better each day through your quiet time. _____
7. It's not important to obey God's Word. _____

Answers
1. True 2. True 3. False 4. False 5. True 6. True 7. False

Look for these verses on pages 63-64 and write on the numbered lines below how you can obey God.

1. Ephesians 4:32
2. 2 Timothy 2:15
3. Matthew 5:44
4. Ephesians 4:28
5. 1 Thessalonians 5:18
6. Philippians 4:4

God wants me to obey Him by:

1. _Being kind and forgiving_
2. _____
3. _____
4. _____
5. _____
6. _____

Ask God to help you obey His Word.

You Can Know That You Are a Witness for God

      Did you know that when the Lord Jesus becomes your Savior, He changes you? The Bible says, "If anyone is in Christ, he is a new creation; the old has gone, the new has come" (2 Corinthians 5:17). As you get to know God better, things in your life will begin to change. You will want to stop doing things that make God unhappy, like lying or fighting with others. Instead you will want to do things that please God, like being a kind and helpful friend.

      As others look at your life, they will start to notice a change in you. When others see that you are loving, kind and honest, or that you have stopped doing the bad things you used to do, they will want to know why you are different.

      You may even have a chance to share with them how God has made a difference in your life. Some of them may want to believe on Jesus as their Savior. Both your actions and your words are a witness, helping others know about Christ.

"... Let your light [life] shine before men, that they may see your good deeds and praise your Father in heaven" (Matthew 5:16).

You Can Know God Will Give You Courage When You Must Suffer for Him

     Sometimes those who have trusted Jesus as their Savior must suffer for Him. Many of God's people have suffered for Jesus down through the years.

     After Jesus returned to Heaven, a young man named Stephen heard about Him and believed. He loved Jesus very much and wanted everyone to know how Jesus died and came alive to pay for their sin. The wicked men who had killed Jesus heard Stephen tell others about Him. They did not want more people to believe, so the men told lies about Stephen. They dragged him out of the city and began to throw stones at him. They kept on throwing big stones until they had killed him.

But God gave Stephen courage and joy even in suffering. Stephen knew that if he died he would be in Heaven with Jesus.

      Maybe you will suffer for Jesus. Maybe your family or friends will be angry and reject you because you believe in Him. Some people may laugh at you or call you bad names.

      Your enemy Satan wants you to become discouraged or get angry with God or give up on Him when others are mean to you because Jesus is your Savior. Instead, when you are suffering for God, you should trust Him for strength to be brave. He will give you courage. God wants you to tell Him about the problem, thank Him for it and wait for Him to work.

Remember that you are not the only one who will suffer for Jesus. Many of God's people have suffered and even died, just as Stephen did. And those who loved God very much were happy that God allowed them to suffer for Him. Ask God for courage and joy as you suffer for Him.

"... if you suffer as a Christian [a believer in Jesus], do not be ashamed, but praise God that you bear that name" (1 Peter 4:16).

You Can Know That Jesus Will Soon Return

  It seems so long ago that Jesus returned to Heaven. Do you wonder when He will come back to earth as He promised? Do you remember how Jesus went back to Heaven? He had given some final instructions to His disciples, then they watched as He went up into the clouds. As the amazed disciples stood watching the sky, two angels came and spoke to them. "Why are you looking up? Jesus is going to come back again, just the way He went up. He will come back in the clouds," the angels said.
  This news made the disciples very happy. They got busy doing the work Jesus had given them to do while they waited for Him to return.
  Many years have gone by since Jesus returned to Heaven and He has not come back yet. But we know that He

will because He promised!

When will Jesus return? No one knows for sure. It could be very soon. What will happen when Jesus returns? The Bible says He will suddenly appear in the clouds with His angels. There will be a loud shout and a trumpet will blow. At that moment, all those who have believed on Jesus as their Savior will rise to meet Him in the clouds. We will all have new bodies that are fit to live in Heaven, where we will live with Him forever.

What should we do while we wait for Jesus to return? We should be busy getting to know God. We should obey Him and help others to know Him too.

"For the Lord himself will come down from heaven, with a loud command, with the voice of the archangel and with the trumpet call of God . . ." (1 Thessalonians 4:16).

Something to think about:

Jesus promised to return someday. Will you be ready to meet Him?

Here are some things you will want to do as you continue learning about God and His plan for your life.

Read your Bible each day.

Pray and talk to God regularly.

Obey His laws.

Worship Him.

Prayer thought for the day:

Thank God for giving you the gift of salvation through Jesus Christ. Don't forget to tell Him how much you love Him.

Bible Verses for

Try to memorize at least one new verse a week.

- [ ] **2 Timothy 2:15** "Do your best to present yourself to God as one approved, a workman who does not need to be ashamed and who correctly handles the word of truth."

- [ ] **Philippians 4:13** "I can do everything through him [God] who gives me strength."

- [ ] **1 John 1:9** "If we confess [admit to God] our sins, he is faithful and just and will forgive us our sins and purify [forgive] us from all unrighteousness [sin]."

- [ ] **1 Thessalonians 5:18** "Give thanks in all circumstances, for this is God's will for you in Christ Jesus."

- [ ] **James 4:7** "Submit yourselves, then, to God. Resist the devil, and he will flee from you."

- [ ] **Philippians 4:4** "Rejoice in the Lord always. I will say it again: Rejoice!"

- [ ] **Ephesians 4:28** "He who has been stealing must steal no longer. . . ."

- [ ] **Hebrews 13:5** ". . . Never will I [God] leave you; never will I forsake you."

- [ ] **Ephesians 4:32** "Be kind and compassionate to one another, forgiving each other, just as in Christ God forgave you."

☐ **1 Corinthians 15:58** "Therefore, my dear brothers, stand firm. Let nothing move you. Always give yourselves fully to the work of the Lord, because you know that your labor in the Lord is not in vain."

☐ **Matthew 5:44** "But I [Jesus] tell you: Love your enemies and pray for those who persecute you."

☐ **1 Corinthians 10:31** "So whether you eat or drink or whatever you do, do it all for the glory of God."

☐ **Isaiah 26:3** "You [God] will keep in perfect peace him whose mind is steadfast, because he trusts in you [God]."

☐ **John 1:12** "Yet to all who received him [Jesus], to those who believed in his name, he gave the right to become children of God."

JOIN THE CLUB

CEF MAILBOX CLUB: Here's your chance to learn more about Jesus through Bible stories and activities that come directly to you in your mailbox! Work at your own pace and send in your answers as you finish each lesson. Complete all eight lessons and you'll receive an official certificate with your name on it. Then go on to complete other lesson series and earn other awards!

If you didn't find the first lesson in the back of your *Wonder Book,* you can ask for one by writing to: **CEF MAILBOX CLUB. 510 Geylang Road. The Sunflower #02-01.Singapore 389466.**

Please include your name and return address.

Copyright© 1998 Child Evangelism Fellowship® Inc.
All rights reserved. No portion of this book may be reproduced in any form without permission from the publisher.

Scripture taken from the HOLY BIBLE, NEW INTERNATIONAL VERSION© NIV®. Copyright© 1973,1978,1984 by the International Bible Society. Used by permission of Zondervan Publishing House. All rights reserved.